THE POWER OF PRAYER

THE POWER OF PRAYER

JUDE HAWTHORNE

CONTENTS

CHAPTER 1

Introduction

The Possibility of Friendship with God

Many people harbor the belief that forming a deep friendship and bond with God is unattainable. This notion, however, is a misconception. Think about it—does the possibility of friendship with God or developing a profound connection belong only to a select few? Doesn't God love all His children equally? The Creator and His creation share a profound bond, one that in some instances manifests as a friendship. God deeply loves His devotees, and this mutual affection is evident throughout religious history.

One remarkable example is the Gopis of Vrindavan, who saw Shri Krishna not just as a deity, but as a friend, relative, or beloved. This divine connection illustrates the nature of a personal and intimate relationship with God. The scriptures affirm this through the saying "iswar anugraha va bhakta sammega," which means that God-realization becomes possible only through God's grace and a heartfelt desire.

The Foundation of a Deep Bond with God

At the core of a deep relationship with God lies an earnest, intense desire to feel His presence. This desire transforms into unwavering faith. When asked to prove the existence of God, an American priest once cleverly retorted, "Do you need to light a bulb to find out whether electricity is flowing through it?" In the same vein, experiencing God's presence requires one to cultivate faith in their heart. As faith strengthens, so does the perception of God's presence in one's life.

Experiencing God's Presence

As a devotee nurtures their faith, they begin to feel God's presence more tangibly. They start to converse with Him, and in turn, God responds in a way that is uniquely understood by the devotee. This personalized communication becomes a dialogue, where the devotee interprets God's guidance as expressions of His will. Over time, this interaction solidifies into a profound friendship. This is reminiscent of the relationship between Arjuna and Shri Krishna during the Mahabharata era—a true testament to divine companionship.

Different Forms of Bonding with God

Typically, a deep bond with God can take various forms. One common form is servitude, where the devotee serves God with immense love and respect. Here, God assumes the role of a caretaker, looking after the welfare of His devotee. Another form is the master-disciple relationship. In this dynamic, the aspirant seeks divine wisdom from God and strives to lead a life imbued with purpose and enlightenment.

CHAPTER 2

Understanding Prayer

Prayer is fundamentally a dialogue—a two-way process of sharing ideas and feelings. This aspect of mutual understanding forms the core of any conversation, including our communication with the Divine.

For anything we undertake, God's will is always relevant, and we are encouraged to seek it through prayer. Importantly, prayers need not be exclusively spiritual; they encompass all aspects of life. This freedom to express our thoughts and feelings to God can be a catalyst for deepening our faith as we recognize His responses and concern, providing us with profound comfort.

God desires an outpouring of our hearts, valuing our innermost thoughts and feelings over mere external words and actions. Our conscience, driven by our thoughts and emotions, ultimately shapes our words and actions. This is why meditation, while valuable for focusing thought, only becomes a conversation with God when it includes speaking to and listening for Him.

Prayer involves the exchange of ideas and feelings. Here lies the beauty and depth of prayer. In private prayer, God is the receiver, and we are the sender. Understanding this dynamic is crucial because it highlights prayer as an exchange with the expectation of a response and true interaction.

Every conversation has a sender and a receiver. For example, when I speak to a friend on the telephone, I am the sender, and my friend is the receiver. Similarly, when I address a large group of people, each person becomes a receiver on a more personal level.

Prayer is simply a conversation with God—a straightforward yet profoundly complex notion. Let's explore what this means in greater detail.

The Nature of Prayer

Prayer encompasses a vast range of human experiences and emotions, reflecting our deepest desires, fears, hopes, and gratitude. It is not confined to formal or structured expressions but includes spontaneous and heartfelt communication with God.

Personal and Communal Prayer

Prayer can be both personal and communal. Personal prayer is an intimate time where we pour out our hearts to God, sharing our deepest thoughts and feelings. Communal prayer, on the other hand, is a collective expression of faith, where individuals come together to seek God's guidance and grace.

The Role of Faith in Prayer

Faith is integral to prayer. It is the trust we place in God's ability to hear and respond to our prayers. As our faith grows, so does our sense of God's presence in our lives. This growing faith is nurtured through regular and sincere prayer, creating a feedback loop where prayer strengthens faith, and faith enriches prayer.

God's Responses

Recognizing God's responses to our prayers requires attentive listening and a heart open to His guidance. God's answers may come in various forms—through scripture, the counsel of others, inner promptings, or the unfolding of circumstances in our lives. Each response is unique to the individual and their relationship with God.

CHAPTER 3

Benefits of Prayer

The Heart of Prayer

This section delves into the myriad reasons why prayer is such a valuable and rewarding practice. It explores the emerging science that reveals how prayer can positively influence various aspects of our lives. This scientific perspective corroborates numerous scriptural references that highlight the benefits of prayer, firmly establishing it as a practical and powerful tool. In a society that often prioritizes tangible outcomes and may offer only superficial attention to prayer, understanding its profound impact is crucial. Prayer is not merely a routine task but an essential investment in our future that deserves top priority.

The Science of Prayer

Recent scientific studies have begun to uncover the effects of prayer on physical, mental, and emotional well-being. Research indicates that prayer can reduce stress, improve mental clarity, and foster a sense of peace. It can also enhance emotional resilience, enabling individuals to navigate life's challenges more effectively. These findings align with scriptural teachings that advocate for regular prayer as a source of strength and guidance.

Practical Benefits

1. **Stress Reduction**: Engaging in prayer can lower stress levels by fostering a sense of calm and serenity. It provides a space to release worries and fears, entrusting them to a higher power.
2. **Emotional Resilience**: Prayer strengthens emotional resilience, helping individuals cope with adversity. By reinforcing a sense of connection and support, it fosters hope and perseverance.
3. **Improved Mental Clarity**: Regular prayer can enhance mental clarity and focus, allowing individuals to approach problems with a clearer, more composed mindset.
4. **Strengthened Relationships**: Prayer can improve relationships by promoting empathy, forgiveness, and understanding. It encourages individuals to reflect on their actions and cultivate virtues that enhance interpersonal connections.

Personal Testimonial

Drawing from the author's personal experiences, this section offers testimonials that make the abstract concept of prayer more tangible. These stories provide encouragement to those who have not yet experienced the transformative power of prayer in their own lives. By sharing real-life examples of how prayer has provided guidance, comfort, and strength, the section illustrates its profound impact.

Personal Stories

To illustrate the benefits of prayer, here are two personal stories demonstrating how prayer can help us through difficult times:

1. **Story of Overcoming Illness**: The author shares a personal account of facing a serious illness. Through fervent prayer, they found peace and strength, which aided their recovery and deepened their faith.

2. **Story of Navigating Financial Hardship**: In times of financial uncertainty, prayer provided the author with clarity and hope. It guided them to make prudent decisions and trust in a positive outcome, eventually leading to stability and growth.

CHAPTER 4

Strengthening Your Prayer Life

Frequent and consistent prayer is immensely beneficial, fostering a mindfulness of God's presence and involvement in your life. This awareness fuels faith and trust. As faith and trust are key indicators of our spiritual life, it stands to reason that strong faith and trust correlate with a robust prayer life, while weak faith and trust arise from infrequent prayer. Therefore, to cultivate a steadfast faith and closer relationship with God, we must develop a stronger prayer habit.

The Importance of a Prayer Habit

Your prayer life is your lifeline of communication with God, a crucial and integral part of your spiritual journey. The apostle Paul emphasizes this in his exhortation to "pray without ceasing" (1 Thessalonians 5:17), which means maintaining an attitude of prayer throughout your day. Additionally, we are encouraged to pray about everything: "Do not be anxious about anything, but in everything, by prayer and petition, with thanksgiving, present your requests to God. And the peace of God, which transcends all understanding, will guard your hearts and minds in Christ Jesus" (Philippians 4:6-7).

Practical Steps to Strengthen Your Prayer Life

1. **Set Regular Prayer Times**: Establish specific times each day dedicated to prayer. Consistency helps build a habit and ensures that prayer becomes a regular part of your daily routine.
2. **Create a Prayer Space**: Designate a quiet, comfortable place for prayer. This space can become a sanctuary where you feel at peace and can focus solely on communicating with God.
3. **Incorporate Different Types of Prayer**: Mix various forms of prayer—such as adoration, confession, thanksgiving, and supplication—to keep your prayer life vibrant and comprehensive.
4. **Use Scripture in Prayer**: Integrate Bible verses into your prayers. This practice not only enriches your prayer experience but also deepens your understanding of God's word.
5. **Keep a Prayer Journal**: Write down your prayers, reflections, and any responses you perceive from God. This journal can serve as a record of your spiritual growth and a source of encouragement.
6. **Pray with Others**: Join a prayer group or find a prayer partner. Praying with others can strengthen your faith and provide support and accountability.

Cultivating an Attitude of Prayer

Beyond structured prayer times, aim to maintain a prayerful mindset throughout your day. This means turning to God in every situation, whether mundane or significant, and recognizing His presence in all aspects of your life. Such an attitude can transform your perspective and bring a sense of peace and guidance.

The Role of Faith and Trust

As your prayer life strengthens, so will your faith and trust in God. These elements are intertwined; as you experience God's presence and responses through prayer, your faith deepens. In turn, this growing faith enhances your prayer life, creating a cycle of spiritual growth and closer communion with God.

CHAPTER 5

Overcoming Challenges in Prayer

The Importance of Perseverance

Perseverance in prayer is a recurrent theme in the Scriptures. Jesus highlighted this in the parable of the unjust judge. This judge, who neither feared God nor respected people, ultimately granted a widow's request for justice due to her persistent pleas. If an unjust judge can be moved by persistence, how much more will a loving God respond to His children?

Biblical Assurance

Jeremiah 29:12-13 offers a beautiful promise: "Then you will call upon me and come and pray to me, and I will listen to you. You will seek me and find me when you seek me with all your heart." This assurance underscores that God desires our communion through prayer and is always ready to respond when we approach Him wholeheartedly.

The Challenges We Face

Prayer, being a powerful tool, faces opposition. Recognizing that prayer strengthens our relationship with God, Satan does everything possible to disrupt it. Distractions, sudden drowsiness, or a wandering mind often emerge just as we begin to pray. These obstacles are subtle yet persistent, making it seem as though anything that can interrupt our prayers will occur.

Recognizing Disruptions

- **Distractions**: It's common to remember tasks or feel an urgent need to do something else as soon as you sit down to pray.
- **Drowsiness**: An overwhelming sense of sleepiness can hit you suddenly during prayer.
- **Wandering Mind**: Your thoughts might drift away from prayer to other concerns or worries.

Strategies to Overcome Challenges

1. **Acknowledge the Distractions**: Recognize that these interruptions are often attempts to prevent you from praying. By understanding their source, you can better address and counter them.
2. **Practice Self-Discipline**: Even when you feel no emotional connection or see no immediate results, continue to pray. Consistency and discipline are key to overcoming these challenges.
3. **Create a Prayer Routine**: Establish a regular prayer schedule and stick to it. Having a routine can help mitigate distractions and create a habit of consistent prayer.
4. **Find a Quiet Space**: Choose a peaceful place for prayer where interruptions are minimal. A designated space can help you focus and maintain a prayerful mindset.
5. **Use Prayer Aids**: Tools like prayer journals, scripture, or written prayers can keep your mind focused and help you stay on track.

6. **Pray for Help**: When you face obstacles in prayer, ask God for assistance. Seeking divine help can strengthen your resolve and bring clarity.

Perseverance in Prayer

To persevere in prayer means to continue despite difficulties, temptations, or feelings of inadequacy. Trusting in God's deliverance and maintaining a steadfast prayer life is crucial. This perseverance is an exercise in faith and trust, reinforcing our spiritual foundation and drawing us closer to God.

CHAPTER 6

Different Forms of Prayer

Understanding the various forms of prayer can enrich your spiritual journey and prevent your prayer life from becoming stagnant. Here, we'll delve into some different types of prayer and how they can be used to deepen your connection with God.

Praying with Scripture

Lectio Divina (Divine Reading): This form of prayer involves reading Scripture slowly and prayerfully, allowing God's Word to speak to your heart. It typically has four steps:

1. **Lectio (Read)**: Read the Scripture passage.
2. **Meditatio (Meditate)**: Reflect on what the passage means to you.
3. **Oratio (Pray)**: Respond to God in prayer.
4. **Contemplatio (Contemplate)**: Rest in God's presence.

Imaginative Prayer

Ignatian Contemplation: Developed by St. Ignatius of Loyola, this form of prayer uses imagination to enter into the Gospel scenes. By visualizing yourself in the biblical story, you engage your senses and emotions, experiencing the presence of God in a vivid and personal way. This method can make Scripture passages come alive and deepen your understanding of Jesus' life.

Vocal Prayer

Spoken or Silent Prayer: Vocal prayer involves speaking to God aloud or in your mind. It can be structured, like the Lord's Prayer, or spontaneous, flowing from your heart. Vocal prayer helps focus your thoughts and can be practiced individually or in community.

Meditative Prayer

Rosary: The Rosary is a form of meditative prayer that involves the repetition of prayers like the Hail Mary, while reflecting on significant events in the lives of Jesus and Mary. This repetitive nature helps to calm the mind and keep it focused on the divine mysteries.

Contemplative Prayer

Centering Prayer: This silent form of prayer emphasizes resting in God's presence. It involves choosing a sacred word and gently focusing on it to center your thoughts on God. Centering prayer can lead to deep inner peace and a sense of God's closeness.

Petitionary Prayer

Asking for Needs: This form of prayer involves bringing your requests before God, seeking His help in various aspects of life. It's a way to express your dependence on Him and your trust in His provision.

Praise and Thanksgiving

Adoration and Gratitude: Praise prayer focuses on adoring God for who He is, while thanksgiving prayer expresses gratitude for His blessings. Both forms cultivate a positive attitude and strengthen your relationship with God by acknowledging His goodness.

Personal Reflection

Journaling: Writing down your prayers and reflections can be a powerful way to communicate with God. It helps to clarify your thoughts and provides a record of your spiritual journey.

Fitting Prayer to Your Life

It's crucial to find forms of prayer that resonate with you and fit your relationship with God at the present time. This understanding prevents your prayer life from becoming a mere routine and helps you avoid forcing yourself into a specific form of prayer that may not be what God is asking of you right now.

CHAPTER 7

Praying with Faith

The Power of Faith

The discovery that faith holds almost magical influence is profound. In various aspects of life, people readily believe the most implausible things, yet they approach faith in God with greater skepticism. Hebrews 11 provides a clear message: faith is what matters to God, not the outcomes. Those who seek God must believe in His existence and trust that He rewards those who earnestly seek Him. Faith, in many ways, represents the final stage of the healing process.

Steps to Develop Faith

Step 1: Trusting God with the Situation The simplest form of faith involves trusting God with our worries and concerns. When we bring our troubles to God and leave them with Him, we demonstrate our belief that God wants to be involved in our lives. This act of trust is a foundational step in nurturing faith.

Step 2: Bothering God about the Problem Contrary to the notion that bothering God with our problems is disrespectful, Scripture shows that God desires our involvement. Jesus' healings and His responses to His disciples indicate that God wants us to bring our troubles to Him and expects us to trust in His intervention. Jesus never turned away anyone who sought healing, illustrating that we should persist in prayer and await God's will.

The Risk of Faith

Praying with faith also involves a level of risk. We must prepare for the discipline of accepting God's will, even if it does not align with our desires. This requires a deep trust in God's plan and a readiness to embrace His outcomes.

Faith as a Healing Process

Faith is integral to the healing process, not just in physical terms but also emotionally and spiritually. By trusting God and involving Him in our problems, we embark on a journey of healing that encompasses all aspects of our being.

CHAPTER 8

Developing a Personal Prayer Routine

Rely on God

When developing a personal prayer routine, the first step is to rely on God and not solely on your own willpower. Be open to surrendering your schedule to what God desires for you. When the deep desire to know God more personally and intensely becomes a resolve that you cannot ignore, you'll know it's time. Until then, make the best use of the time you have, knowing that Jesus understands human limitations. He offers grace to those who are humble, so be patient with yourself as you learn to depend on Him.

Start with Realistic Goals

If you're new to Christianity or have never established a daily quiet time, it's essential to set realistic goals. It's not advisable to immediately cancel all social events, delay daily responsibilities, or stay up late to achieve a quiet time. Such drastic changes could lead to burnout and frustration. Developing a prayer routine is a gradual process, not a sprint. Start small and allow yourself to grow into a more disciplined prayer life.

Setting Clear Goals

Using a prayer journal can be incredibly helpful. Write down a clear and heartfelt aim for your prayer life. For instance, you might set a goal like: "One year from today, I want to have an established daily quiet time that includes reading the entire Bible and praying for at least half an hour each day." Realize that it will take time to develop this discipline, and you might need to adjust your goals along the way. Regularly evaluating your progress can help you stay on track.

Practical Tips for a Prayer Routine

1. **Start Small**: Begin with a short amount of time and gradually increase it as you become more comfortable. Even five minutes a day can be a solid start.
2. **Create a Schedule**: Choose a specific time each day for prayer and stick to it. Consistency helps build a habit.
3. **Find a Quiet Place**: A peaceful environment can help you focus and eliminate distractions.
4. **Be Flexible**: Life can be unpredictable. If you miss a scheduled prayer time, don't be discouraged. Find another time during the day to connect with God.
5. **Use Prayer Tools**: Prayer journals, devotional books, or apps can provide structure and inspiration.
6. **Incorporate Scripture**: Reading the Bible during your prayer time can deepen your understanding and connection with God.
7. **Seek Accountability**: Share your prayer goals with a trusted friend or join a prayer group. Encouragement and accountability can be powerful motivators.

The Journey of Prayer

Remember, developing a prayer routine is a journey. It requires patience, persistence, and a willingness to adjust as needed. Trust that God is with you every step of the way, and He honors your efforts to draw closer to Him.

CHAPTER 9

Deepening Your Relationship with God

The Two-Way Communication

To deepen your relationship with God, it is essential to understand that it involves a two-way process of communication. It's not enough to only speak to God through prayer; we must also learn to listen to Him. This requires attuning ourselves to His presence in our lives, which can often be a quiet and gentle influence, easily drowned out by the noise and haste of modern life.

Developing the Skill of Listening

Patience is crucial when learning to listen to God's voice. Spending time in prayerful solitude and silence, whether in nature or in the quiet moments of the morning, provides the opportunity to develop this skill. Keeping a journal can be helpful during this time. Writing down thoughts, feelings, and whatever you sense God is saying to you can provide clarity and insight. This form of prayer allows you to reflect and later share your experiences with a spiritual director or mentor.

The Heart of Prayer

At the core of our prayer life is the desire to foster and develop our relationship with God. Relationships grow and develop over time through complex interactions. Similarly, we aim to grow and deepen our relationship with God through various means.

Ways to Foster Your Relationship with God

- **Communication**: Regular and heartfelt communication with God through prayer is fundamental.
- **Learning about God**: Spending time reading Scripture and other spiritual texts helps us learn more about God and His will for us.
- **Spending Time Together**: Dedicate time each day to be with God, whether in prayer, meditation, or contemplation.
- **Sharing Common Tasks**: Involve God in your daily activities by offering your work and tasks to Him.
- **Resolving Conflicts**: Seek God's guidance in resolving personal conflicts and misunderstandings.
- **Expressing Feelings**: Share your feelings of love, adoration, gratitude, and even sorrow with God.

Integrating Forms of Prayer

In the following sections, we will explore how these ways of fostering a relationship with God can be translated into specific forms of prayer. These forms are not meant to be viewed in isolation but are deeply interrelated and can be used concurrently towards the same end.

1. **Communication and Vocal Prayer**: Speaking to God openly and honestly about your thoughts and needs.
2. **Learning and Meditative Prayer**: Reflecting on Scripture and spiritual texts to gain a deeper understanding of God's will.

3. **Time Together and Contemplative Prayer**: Spending quiet time in God's presence, resting in His love.
4. **Sharing Tasks and Petitionary Prayer**: Offering your daily tasks to God and asking for His guidance.
5. **Conflict Resolution and Intercessory Prayer**: Seeking God's help in resolving conflicts and praying for others.
6. **Expressing Feelings and Praise**: Using prayer to express your love, gratitude, and adoration for God.

CHAPTER 10

Cultivating a Spirit of Gratitude

The Awareness of God's Presence

For those who are acquainted with God through prayer, a spirit of thankfulness often arises from the quiet awareness of His presence. The Holy Spirit's prompting in prayer brings believers to new and deeper realizations of God's grace, mercy, and saving love in Christ. As believers reflect on the abundance of God's blessings, they naturally respond with heartfelt joy and gratitude.

Transformative Power of Gratitude

The Spirit of God brings about inner transformation, pulling individuals away from self-centeredness, rebellion, and ingratitude. This transformation draws them closer to God in a spirit of loving adoration and thankfulness, fostering a desire to be in His presence.

Gratitude as an Attitude

Gratitude is fundamentally an attitude that recognizes life as a gift, promoting a general feeling of thankfulness. This attitude should be a constant in our prayers. Developing gratitude is crucial for connecting with God because a thankful heart aligns with God's will. As the apostle Paul instructs in 1 Thessalonians 5:16-18, "Be joyful always; pray continually; give thanks in all circumstances, for this is God's will for you in Christ Jesus."

The Role of Gratitude

- **Attuned to God**: Thankfulness keeps us attuned to God and acts as a barrier against sins like pride, covetousness, and greed.
- **Reflecting on Past Events**: Reflecting on past experiences helps us recognize the times when God has significantly impacted our lives. It often reveals how we may have neglected to give thanks during good times, turning to God only during hardships.
- **Living Out Faith**: A person who is consciously aware of God's presence will express their faith and gratitude in every action, making thankfulness a way of life.

Practical Steps to Cultivate Gratitude

1. **Daily Reflection**: Spend time each day reflecting on the blessings in your life and expressing gratitude for them.
2. **Keep a Gratitude Journal**: Write down things you are thankful for each day. This practice can help you maintain a thankful attitude.
3. **Prayer of Thanksgiving**: Incorporate prayers of thanksgiving into your daily routine. Thank God for His grace, mercy, and the many gifts He has bestowed upon you.
4. **Practice Mindfulness**: Be mindful of God's presence in your daily life and acknowledge His role in the events and circumstances you encounter.
5. **Share Your Gratitude**: Express your thankfulness to others. Sharing your gratitude can inspire and uplift those around you.

By fostering a spirit of gratitude, we align our hearts with God's will and deepen our relationship with Him. Thankfulness becomes a natural response to His presence and blessings in our lives.

CHAPTER 11

Praying for Guidance and Wisdom

A **Prayer for Guidance**

Here's an example of how to seek God's guidance for wisdom and help in decision-making:

> **O Lord, I know that the way of man is not in himself. It is not in man who walks to direct his own steps (Jeremiah 10:23). We know this from experience! We have all failed dismally in making decisions apart from You, and many of us have suffered the painful consequences of going our own way. So we come to You, Father, and place this important decision into Your hands. You have promised that if any of us lacks wisdom, we should ask of God, who gives to all liberally and without reproach, and it will be given to him (James 1:5). How we praise You for such a promise! And we are claiming it now. We desire so much for this decision to be based on Your wisdom and Your leading. We ask that through Your Son, God, you will make this decision known to us. For we know that our flesh is weak and we desire our own way. O Lord, prevent us from moving ahead if this is not Your will. We are willing to wait and even endure not having what we so much desire,**

rather than step out in front of You. So shut or open the doors as You see fit. And if at any time we are to deviate to the right hand or to the left, we shall hear Your voice behind us saying, "This is the way, walk in it." We are claiming this promise! (Isaiah 30:21-22).

Seeking God's Guidance

When faced with important decisions, it's crucial not to lean solely on our understanding. It's easy to be swayed by our desires and rush into wrong choices. At such times, seeking God's guidance becomes vital. God, who knows all possible outcomes, is more than willing to direct our paths if we earnestly seek Him.

Methods of Receiving Guidance

- **Through Circumstances**: Sometimes, God's direction becomes clear through the unfolding of events around us.
- **Through Other People**: God often speaks through the counsel of trusted friends, mentors, or spiritual advisors.
- **Through the Word of God**: Regular reading and meditation on Scripture can provide clarity and insight into God's will.
- **Through Inner Conviction**: A sense of inner peace or an unmistakable conviction can be God's way of guiding us.

Assurance of God's Guidance

Isaiah 58:11 assures us that "The Lord will guide you always; He will satisfy your needs in a sun-scorched land and will strengthen your frame." This promise reassures us that as we seek God's direction, He will faithfully guide us along the right path.

CHAPTER 12

Finding Peace through Prayer

When peace seems elusive, it's crucial to turn to God, our ultimate source of comfort and strength. Prayer can help us achieve the peace that God desires for our lives. Here are some practical steps to finding peace through prayer:

1. Understanding Life's Transience

Recognize that this world is not our ultimate home. Some things will only be made right in the next life. Embracing this truth can bring peace even in the midst of trials, as it reminds us of the bigger picture and the eternal hope we have in God.

2. Laying Burdens on God

Cast your burdens on God, knowing that He cares for you. Truly letting go of worries and placing them in God's hands requires trust. Often, continued worry indicates a lack of trust in God's ability to handle our problems. Practice surrendering your concerns to Him completely.

3. Trusting God Through Trials

Understand that God sometimes allows us to endure trials to draw us closer to Him. Through these challenges, we learn what genuine trust in God looks like. This deep trust, cultivated through life's difficulties, can bring profound peace.

4. Deepening Knowledge and Trust

Develop trust and understanding by knowing God better. He has given us His word to help us achieve this. Reading the Psalms, for instance, can reveal God's nature and character. Understanding His unconditional love and grace towards His children makes it easier to trust Him, bringing peace to our hearts.

Practical Steps to Cultivate Peace Through Prayer

1. **Daily Reflection**: Set aside time each day to reflect on God's promises and His presence in your life.
2. **Scripture Reading**: Regularly read the Bible, especially passages like the Psalms that highlight God's faithfulness and love.
3. **Gratitude Practice**: Keep a gratitude journal to record the blessings in your life and thank God for them.
4. **Surrender Prayer**: Make it a habit to surrender your worries and concerns to God in prayer each day.
5. **Trust Exercises**: During trials, consciously remind yourself of times when God has been faithful and has seen you through difficult situations.

By implementing these steps and maintaining a consistent prayer life, you can experience the peace that surpasses all understanding, even in the midst of life's challenges.

CHAPTER 13

Praying for Healing and Restoration

When we pray for healing and restoration, we are seeking God's intervention to restore health and wholeness in our lives or the lives of others. Healing refers to being restored to health, whether physically, emotionally, or spiritually. Restoration means being brought back to a former or original state, indicating a return to wholeness.

Biblical Basis for Healing and Restoration

A notable example of this is found in Malachi 4:2: "But for you who revere my name, the sun of righteousness will rise with healing in its wings." This scripture speaks broadly about the healing that accompanies salvation, but it can also be interpreted as referring to physical healing. While believers are not guaranteed perfect health at all times, God is both able and willing to heal, and we should feel encouraged to ask Him for healing for ourselves and others.

How to Pray for Healing and Restoration

Express Your Needs to God: Start by honestly presenting your needs and the needs of others to God. Recognize His power and willingness to heal.

Claim God's Promises: Like in James 1:5, where God promises to give wisdom generously to those who ask, we can trust that He hears our prayers for healing. Believers can approach God with confidence, claiming His promises for healing and restoration.

Surrender to God's Will: While praying for healing, it's essential to submit to God's will, recognizing that His plans and timing are perfect, even if they differ from our desires.

Trust in God's Provision: Develop trust in God's ability to bring healing and restoration. Reflect on past experiences and biblical examples where God's healing power was evident.

Continue in Faith and Patience: Perseverance in prayer is crucial. Maintain your faith even if the healing does not happen immediately. Trust that God is working in ways that may not be immediately visible.

Practical Steps to Pray for Healing

1. **Identify the Need**: Clearly identify what needs healing or restoration, whether it's physical, emotional, or spiritual.
2. **Pray with Specificity**: Pray specifically for the areas where healing is needed, mentioning the person or situation by name.
3. **Incorporate Scripture**: Use relevant scriptures in your prayers to reinforce your faith and trust in God's promises.
4. **Join with Others**: If possible, pray with others. Corporate prayer can be powerful and provide additional support and encouragement.
5. **Reflect and Listen**: Spend time in quiet reflection, listening for God's guidance and assurance.

Example Prayer for Healing and Restoration

> Heavenly Father, we come before You with hearts full of faith, seeking Your healing touch. You are the Great Physician, capable of mending all wounds and restoring us to health. We lift up those who are in need of Your healing, whether it be physical, emotional, or spiritual. According to Your promise in Malachi 4:2, we ask that You bring healing in Your wings. We trust in Your power and mercy, believing that You hear our cries and will respond according to Your perfect will. Help us to surrender our worries and fears to You, and to trust in Your divine plan. May Your peace and healing flow through us, bringing restoration and wholeness. In Jesus' name, we pray. Amen.

By consistently praying in this manner, we can draw closer to God and witness His healing power in our lives.

CHAPTER 14

Seeking Forgiveness through Prayer

Acknowledging Sins
The journey of seeking forgiveness begins with an honest and humble acknowledgment of our sins before God. It is through sincere prayer that we confess our wrongdoings and ask for His forgiveness. This is a deeply personal and private act of contrition and repentance.

Misunderstandings About Forgiveness

Many people have misconceptions about the process of seeking forgiveness. Some believe that publicly declaring their sins or seeking forgiveness from those against whom they have sinned increases their chances of being forgiven. However, this can sometimes exacerbate the situation, leading to further indiscretions and misunderstandings.

Preserving Dignity

It's crucial to understand that no one should hastily reveal their past transgressions to others. Such revelations can not only lead others into similar sins but can also trivialize the gravity of the sin itself. Protecting the dignity of the sinner is paramount, and the process of seeking forgiveness should be a private matter between the individual and God.

Making Amends

Instead of public confessions, individuals should seek to make amends privately with God. This involves heartfelt repentance and a sincere desire to change one's ways. It is through this private communion with God that true forgiveness and restoration are sought.

A Prayer for Forgiveness

Here's an example of a prayer seeking God's forgiveness:

> **O Merciful God, I come before You with a contrite heart, acknowledging my sins and seeking Your forgiveness. I am deeply sorry for my transgressions and ask for Your mercy and grace. Help me to turn away from my sinful ways and to live a life that is pleasing to You. Grant me the strength to make amends and to seek reconciliation where possible. Thank You for Your boundless love and forgiveness. In Your holy name, I pray. Amen.**

Steps to Seek Forgiveness

1. **Private Confession**: Confess your sins directly to God in a private and sincere manner.
2. **Heartfelt Repentance**: Truly repent for your actions, showing a genuine desire to change.
3. **Seek God's Guidance**: Ask for God's guidance and strength to avoid future transgressions.
4. **Make Amends**: Where possible, make amends with those affected by your actions, but do so in a manner that maintains dignity and respect.

Praying for Others

The Power of Intercessory Prayer

Ezekiel provides a striking example of God's openness to intercessory prayer. In Ezekiel 22:30-31, God states that He searched for someone "to build up the wall and stand in the gap before Me for the land, so that I would not destroy it, but I found no one. Thus I have poured out My indignation on them; I have consumed them with the fire of My wrath; their way I have brought upon their heads." This passage highlights the significant role intercessory prayer can play in preventing destruction and invoking God's mercy, even though in this instance, no one interceded.

Understanding Anthropopathism

These verses are anthropopathic, meaning they describe God in human terms to make them easier for us to understand. While not literally true, they illustrate that God takes intercessory prayer seriously and that such prayers can indeed influence outcomes.

Intercessory Prayer as an Act of Love

Praying for others is a profound act of love. Through intercessory prayer, we become channels for God's grace, bringing healing and support into others' lives. God often desires to spare people from the consequences of their sins, as seen in numerous scriptural examples.

Biblical Examples of Intercessory Prayer

- **Moses' Intercession**: In response to Moses' plea on behalf of the Israelites, "The LORD changed His mind" (Exodus 32:14). This shows that earnest intercession can lead to divine mercy.
- **Prophet Jeremiah**: Conversely, in Jeremiah 7:16 and 14:11, God instructs the prophet not to pray for the people, indicating that sometimes, in His perfect knowledge, God's judgment is unchangeable. However, these instances still underscore the potential power of intercessory prayer to influence God's decisions.

How to Pray for Others

1. **Identify Specific Needs**: Clearly identify the needs of the person or situation you are praying for.
2. **Pray with Empathy**: Approach God with a heart full of empathy and compassion for those you are interceding for.
3. **Use Scripture**: Incorporate relevant Bible verses to reinforce your prayers and align them with God's promises.
4. **Be Persistent**: Continue to pray consistently and fervently, trusting that God hears your prayers.
5. **Trust God's Wisdom**: While praying for others, trust in God's ultimate wisdom and plan, even if the answers do not come in the way you expect.

Example of an Intercessory Prayer

> Heavenly Father, we come before You with hearts full of compassion, lifting up [Name] to You. We ask for Your grace and healing to flow into their life. According to Your word in James 5:16, we know that the prayer of a righteous person is powerful and effective. We pray for Your mercy and inter-

vention in their situation, believing in Your power to restore and renew. Guide them with Your wisdom and surround them with Your peace. In Jesus' name, we pray. Amen.

The Power of Intercessory Prayer

Intercessory prayer is a powerful and effective form of prayer where one acts as a mediator, seeking to reconcile differences and bring others closer to God. The term "intercede" means to mediate or intervene on behalf of another. The apostle Paul highlights this in 2 Corinthians 5:20: "We are ambassadors for Christ, as though God were making entreaty through us; we beg you on behalf of Christ, be reconciled to God." This passage underscores the role of believers in interceding for others, urging them to be reconciled to God.

The Highest Calling

Intercessory prayer, next to the redemptive work of Christ, is considered one of the highest callings a believer can undertake. It involves selflessly praying on behalf of others, regardless of their spiritual status, and consistently mediating before God for their needs. This form of prayer is a vital aspect of Christian ministry, accessible to all who genuinely desire to serve others.

Spiritual Opposition in Prayer

Those engaged in prominent ministries often experience the greatest spiritual opposition not during their active ministry but during times of prayer. This is because effective prayer, which speaks truth and liberates people from spiritual bondage, poses a significant threat to Satan. The effectiveness of Christ working through believers is what Satan aims to thwart. As Christ stated in Matthew 16:18, "the gates of Hell shall not prevail against the Church." Therefore, greater spiritual attacks require stronger defenses through prayer, with intercessory prayer being the most powerful spiritual defense available.

The Role of Intercessory Prayer

Intercessory prayer plays a crucial role in Christian ministry, serving as a means to:

- **Mediate for Others**: Acting as intermediaries between God and those in need, seeking reconciliation and healing.
- **Address Spiritual Needs**: Directly addressing the spiritual challenges and needs of others through prayer.
- **Provide Spiritual Defense**: Offering robust spiritual protection against attacks from the enemy.
- **Empower Ministries**: Supporting and empowering various forms of ministry through consistent prayer support.

The Effectiveness of Intercessory Prayer

Intercessory prayer has a profound impact on both the person praying and those being prayed for. It aligns the prayer warrior with God's will, deepening their spiritual connection and dependence on Him. For those being prayed for, it can bring about healing, deliverance, and spiritual growth.

How to Engage in Intercessory Prayer

1. **Identify Needs**: Recognize and understand the specific needs of those you are praying for.

2. **Pray Consistently**: Maintain regular and persistent prayer for these needs.
3. **Use Scripture**: Incorporate biblical promises and truths in your prayers to reinforce faith.
4. **Stay Humble and Dependable**: Approach prayer with a humble heart, fully relying on God's power and wisdom.
5. **Seek God's Guidance**: Continually ask for God's guidance on how best to pray and support those in need.

Intercessory prayer is a powerful expression of love and faith, creating a spiritual lifeline that connects individuals to God's grace and mercy.

CHAPTER 17

Praying for Strength and Courage

When faced with overwhelming situations, praying for strength and courage becomes vital. Your experience in a dangerous situation where you asked God for help and felt His presence is a powerful testament to the efficacy of such prayers. These prayers are often made when we feel overpowered and uncertain about how to confront the challenges ahead.

The Need for Strength and Courage

In today's society, we are constantly bombarded with news of war, violence, and inner pain. These events, even if they do not directly involve us, can deeply affect our sense of peace and security. Praying for strength and courage helps us find the resilience needed to navigate these turbulent times.

A Personal Example of Prayer for Strength

Here is an example of a prayer for strength and courage based on your experience:

> **Dear Lord, I am faced with a situation that fills me with fear and uncertainty. I know I cannot handle this on my own, so I turn to You, asking for Your strength and courage. Help me to keep a clear head and stay close to You. Thank You for**

hearing my prayer and for the peace that surpasses all under-standing. Amen.

Practical Steps to Praying for Strength

1. **Acknowledge Your Fear**: Admit to God that you are afraid and need His help.
2. **Ask for Specific Help**: Pray for clarity, courage, and the ability to stay calm.
3. **Trust in God's Presence**: Have faith that God is with you, providing the strength you need.
4. **Reflect on Past Experiences**: Remember previous times when God has answered your prayers, reinforcing your trust in Him.
5. **Stay Persistent in Prayer**: Continue to pray, even when the situation is overwhelming.

The Impact of Prayer

Consistent prayer can bring about a sense of peace and reduced fear, as you experienced. This sense of peace is a testament to the strength and courage that God provides when we ask Him in faith.

CHAPTER 18

Praying for Provision and Blessings

The Assurance of Asking

It is comforting to know that when we find ourselves in need, all we have to do is ask God. Many people might not always be certain about what they want or need in life, but they are often aware of their unmet needs. Asking God for guidance and blessings to fulfill these necessities is a crucial step. James 4:2-3 emphasizes that sometimes we do not have because we do not ask, or when we ask, we do not receive because our motives are not aligned with God's will.

Aligning Motives with God's Will

James 4:2-3 teaches us about the importance of asking with the right intentions. It suggests that we must approach God with humility, seeking provision not out of selfish desires but in alignment with His will. Similarly, 1 John 5:14-15 assures us that God hears us when we ask for anything that pleases Him, and we can be confident that He will grant our requests if they align with His will.

Understanding Provision

Provision refers to the necessities required for our daily lives. When we pray for provision and blessings, we are seeking the fulfillment of our immediate and future needs, trusting in God's abundance. In Matthew 6:11, Jesus teaches us to pray, "Give us this day our daily bread," reminding us to rely on God for our daily sustenance and needs, no matter how big or small.

Practical Steps to Pray for Provision

1. **Identify Your Needs**: Clearly identify what you need and present these needs to God in prayer.
2. **Align Your Motives**: Ensure that your requests align with God's will, seeking His guidance and blessings with a humble heart.
3. **Trust in God's Promise**: Have faith in God's promise that He will provide for our needs when we ask according to His will.
4. **Express Gratitude**: Always thank God for His provisions and blessings, acknowledging His grace and mercy in your life.

Example of a Prayer for Provision

> **Heavenly Father, I come before You with a humble heart, seeking Your guidance and provision. You know my needs, both immediate and future, and I trust in Your promise to supply them. Help me to align my desires with Your will and to seek Your blessings with pure motives. I ask for Your provision and blessings, trusting that You will provide according to Your perfect plan. Thank You for Your unwavering love and grace. In Jesus' name, I pray. Amen.**

By consistently praying in this manner and trusting in God's provision, we can experience His abundant blessings in our lives.

CHAPTER 19

Praying in Times of Crisis

In times of crisis, distress can be particularly intense, making it difficult to feel God's presence. When disaster strikes and we turn to God in prayer, it can sometimes feel as though He is remote, absent, or even responsible for the trouble. This can lead to feelings of being let down. However, it is precisely during these times of severe trouble that we must intensify our efforts to bring everything before God in prayer.

The Example of Nehemiah

God's servant, Nehemiah, provides an exemplary model of concern and leadership during a crisis. He asked God to remember his faithfulness and to help him during difficult times, even though God had never failed him. Nehemiah's approach teaches us to persist in prayer, presenting our concerns logically and methodically to God. Like a watchman who stands guard day and night, we should persist in prayer until the desired answer comes.

Asking for God's Explanation

With great pastoral sensitivity, Lloyd-Jones reminds us that it is perfectly acceptable to ask God to explain His actions and purposes. However, we must be prepared to face the truth and to be further enlightened by His response. This openness to God's guidance and understanding can bring peace and clarity during times of crisis.

Practical Steps for Praying in Crisis

1. **Acknowledge Your Feelings**: Admit to God your feelings of fear, confusion, or even anger. Being honest about your emotions can help you connect more deeply in prayer.
2. **Persist in Prayer**: Continue to pray consistently, even when you feel overwhelmed. Like Nehemiah, keep presenting your concerns to God with faith and determination.
3. **Seek Understanding**: Ask God to explain His actions and purposes, and be open to His guidance and truth. Trust that He will enlighten you in His own time and way.
4. **Find Comfort in Scripture**: Reflect on biblical examples of people who faced crises and found strength in God. Their stories can provide encouragement and perspective.
5. **Stay Connected to Community**: Lean on your faith community for support and prayer. Sharing your burdens with others can provide additional strength and comfort.

Example Prayer in Times of Crisis

> **Heavenly Father, in this time of crisis, I come to You with a heavy heart. I feel overwhelmed and uncertain, and I struggle to sense Your presence. Please give me the strength and courage to persist in prayer. Help me to trust in Your wisdom and guidance. I ask for Your peace to calm my troubled heart and for Your light to guide me through this dark time. I also ask that You explain Your actions and purposes, so that I may be further enlightened and find peace in Your plan. In Jesus' name, I pray. Amen.**

By persistently bringing your concerns to God and seeking His guidance, you can find the strength and peace needed to navigate through times of crisis.

CHAPTER 20

Maintaining Consistency in Prayer

The Challenge of Time Management

One of the biggest obstacles to consistent prayer is proper time management. Often, it seems like there is no time to pray amidst the busyness of daily life. However, there is always time for things deemed important. Unfortunately, many do not prioritize prayer as much as other daily activities. To recapture the importance of prayer, consider the consequences of living without constant communion with God. We are commanded to pray continually, and neglecting this can cause us to lose touch with God's will, leading to decisions made without His guidance, which can be damaging to ourselves and others.

Understanding the Importance of Prayer

Recognizing the implications and consequences of not praying can help us place a greater priority on prayer. Living without consistent prayer means missing out on God's guidance and wisdom in our lives. When we understand that prayer is essential for maintaining a close relationship with God, we are more likely to make it a priority.

Practical Tips for Consistent Prayer

1. **Integrate Prayer into Daily Routine**: Look for opportunities throughout the day to pray. This could be during a commute, while doing household chores, or during a break at work. Integrating prayer into your daily routine ensures you stay connected with God consistently.

2. **Engage in Mental Prayer**: Even when it's not feasible to stop and say a prayer out loud, engage in mental prayer. While at work or in a meeting, think about the situation you're praying for and lift it up to God in your mind. This keeps you connected to God throughout the day.

3. **Set Specific Times for Prayer**: Designate specific times for prayer each day. Setting aside dedicated time helps establish a habit. It could be early in the morning, during lunch, or before bed.

4. **Use Reminders**: Write notes or set alarms on your phone to remind yourself to pray. Having a visual or audible reminder can help you remember to take time to pray, even on busy days.

5. **Prioritize Prayer**: Make prayer a priority by understanding its significance. Remind yourself of the benefits of consistent prayer and how it aligns you with God's will.

Example Prayer for Maintaining Consistency

> **Heavenly Father, I come to You seeking help in maintaining a consistent prayer life. I recognize the importance of staying connected with You and the consequences of neglecting prayer. Please guide me in managing my time effectively so that I can prioritize prayer. Help me to integrate prayer into my daily routine and to engage in mental prayer when I cannot pray out loud. Remind me to set specific times for prayer**

and to use reminders if needed. Thank You for Your constant presence in my life. In Jesus' name, I pray. Amen.

By implementing these practical tips and understanding the importance of prayer, you can maintain a consistent prayer life and stay connected with God's will for your life.

CHAPTER 21

Overcoming Distractions in Prayer

Distractions during prayer are a common challenge, but they can be overcome with persistence and intentional practices. Here are some practical steps and insights to help maintain focus during your conversation with God:

Bringing Thoughts Back Gently

When you find your mind wandering, gently but persistently bring your thoughts back to your prayer. Don't be harsh on yourself; instead, guide your focus back to God with patience.

Using Imagination and Thought

Some people find it helpful to use their imagination to create a mental space for prayer. For instance, Petrarch, the 14th-century Italian poet, would visualize a firm and ordered council to collect his thoughts. In your mind, create a quiet, serene place where you can retreat and focus solely on your conversation with God.

Fixed Periods of Positive Attention

Set aside specific periods for focused prayer. For example, dedicate five minutes solely to offering your full attention to God. As you practice this regularly, you'll find it easier to extend these periods and reduce the frequency and duration of distractions.

Keeping a Record

Track your prayer sessions and note when distractions occur. This helps you identify patterns and work on minimizing them. Over time, you'll see improvement in your ability to maintain focus during prayer.

Embracing the Challenge

Overcoming distractions sometimes requires persistence and effort. An old and infirm man who was praised for his regular prayer life explained that it took him years of consistent effort to reach a point where prayer required no effort. Understand that this is a journey, and every effort you make brings you closer to a more focused and meaningful prayer life.

Practical Steps to Minimize Distractions

1. **Create a Prayer Space**: Find a quiet, comfortable place for prayer where you are less likely to be disturbed.
2. **Set Specific Times**: Schedule regular prayer times and stick to them, making it a consistent part of your routine.
3. **Use Prayer Aids**: Tools like prayer beads, prayer books, or guided meditations can help maintain focus.
4. **Incorporate Scripture**: Reading a Bible passage before prayer can help center your thoughts.
5. **Mindfulness Practices**: Techniques such as deep breathing or mindfulness exercises can help calm the mind before prayer.

The Reward of Perseverance

Persevering through distractions can lead to a deeper, more joyful, and peaceful prayer life. Remember that all believers face trials and temptations, but those who persist in their efforts will ultimately experience the fullness of God's presence.

CHAPTER 22

Deepening Your Spiritual Connection

Enhancing your spiritual connection is a profound and rewarding journey. Here are several practical steps to help develop greater spirituality:

Daily Reflection and Meditation

Set aside time each day to be alone with your thoughts. Use this time to meditate, ponder, and pray. This practice helps you center yourself and connect more deeply with your spiritual beliefs.

Regular Worship Attendance

Attend a temple, church, or other place of worship regularly. While attendance alone does not guarantee spiritual experience, consistently spending time in a sacred place can positively influence your life and behavior.

Conscious Decision-Making

Make a conscious decision to refrain from doing things you know are wrong. Acting in violation of God's laws can hinder your spiritual growth. Every decision to do right, no matter how small, leads to greater spiritual awareness and a more god-like life.

Immersion in Uplifting Literature

Immerse yourself in good literature. Reading and listening to uplifting and inspiring content can enrich your mind and spirit, fostering a deeper connection with your faith.

Acts of Service

Take more time to help others. Serving your fellow beings is one of the most direct ways to emulate God's love and compassion. Engaging in acts of service can significantly deepen your spiritual connection.

Guarding and Nurturing Your Spiritual Connection

Remember that your spiritual connection is precious. Guard it carefully and be faithful in nurturing it. Deepening your spiritual connection involves consistent actions that enhance your knowledge of and relationship with the Divine. It is a long-term effort, but one that brings great satisfaction and joy.

Practical Steps to Implement These Ideas

1. **Set a Routine**: Schedule specific times for reflection, meditation, and prayer each day.
2. **Commit to Regular Worship**: Make attending worship services a non-negotiable part of your routine.
3. **Make Ethical Choices**: Consciously choose actions that align with your spiritual values.
4. **Engage with Uplifting Content**: Choose books, music, and media that inspire and uplift your spirit.
5. **Volunteer and Serve**: Find opportunities to serve others in your community or through your place of worship.

Example of a Daily Prayer for Spiritual Growth

> **Dear Heavenly Father, I come before You seeking to deepen my spiritual connection with You. Help me to set aside time each day to reflect, meditate, and pray. Guide me to make**

ethical choices and refrain from actions that violate Your laws. May I immerse myself in uplifting literature and find joy in serving others. Protect and nurture my spiritual connection, and grant me the strength and wisdom to grow closer to You each day. In Your holy name, I pray. Amen.

By consistently applying these principles, you can cultivate a richer and more fulfilling spiritual life.

CHAPTER 23

The Role of Scripture in Prayer

Scripture as a Gift of God

Scripture is a divine gift, inspired and preserved by God, given to His people as a means of grace. It is the Word of God expressed through human language, leading us to salvation in Christ and equipping us for every good work. As such, Scripture is sufficient for all aspects of life and serves as the foundation of our Christian prayers.

Praying with Scripture

Scripture provides both the material and the appropriate way to express our thoughts and desires to God. When we use the words of Scripture in our prayers, we are praying in the Spirit, with the Word, and with understanding. This practice allows us to align our prayers with God's will and deepen our spiritual connection.

Turning Scripture into Prayer

Sometimes, in our weakness, we struggle to find the words to pray. We may feel tongue-tied or unsure of what to pray for. In such moments, turning to the Psalms or other Scriptures that resonate with our thoughts and feelings can be incredibly helpful. By praying the very words of Scripture, we can express our deepest emotions and desires to God.

Practical Steps to Incorporate Scripture into Prayer

1. **Daily Scripture Reading**: Make it a habit to read the Bible daily. Select passages that speak to your heart and reflect on them.
2. **Use Psalms in Prayer**: The Book of Psalms is particularly rich in prayers and praises. Find a Psalm that resonates with your current feelings and pray it to God.
3. **Memorize Scripture**: Commit key verses to memory. These verses can be recalled and prayed during times of need.
4. **Journal Prayers**: Write down Scriptures that stand out to you and use them as a basis for your prayers. Journaling helps in reflecting and deepening your understanding.
5. **Reflect and Meditate**: Take time to meditate on the Scriptures. Let the words sink in and guide your prayers.

Example of Praying with Scripture

Here's an example of how to turn a passage from the Psalms into a prayer:

> **Psalm 23:1-3** > "The Lord is my shepherd; I shall not want. He makes me lie down in green pastures. He leads me beside still waters. He restores my soul."

> **Prayer:** > Dear Lord, You are my shepherd, and I trust that I shall not want. Thank You for leading me to green pastures and still waters, where I find peace and restoration. Restore my soul, O Lord, and guide me in Your paths of righteousness. Amen.

By incorporating Scripture into our prayers, we draw closer to God and find a deeper, more meaningful way to communicate with Him.

CHAPTER 24

Praying with Humility and Surrender

Humility in Prayer

God resists our pride because it places us in His position. Humility is about putting God in His rightful place. As Peter instructs us, we must humble ourselves under the mighty hand of God (1 Peter 5:6-7). One way to do this is by casting all our worries, fears, and concerns upon Him in prayer, demonstrating our trust that He is capable and willing to take care of everything. When we come to God with our burdens and lay them at His feet, we exhibit humility and faith. Conversely, trying to handle things ourselves, even after asking God for help, shows pride and unbelief, undermining the process of prayer.

True Surrender

There is a significant difference between asking God to take care of things while expecting Him to do our bidding, and truly letting go of control and submitting to His will. A humble, surrendered spirit is crucial for staying connected to God through prayer. If we're not careful, the very act of prayer can become an expression of pride. Sometimes we believe that if we push and shove hard enough, we can get God to do what we want. This mindset turns prayer into a futile attempt to manipulate an Almighty God.

Letting Go

We may cry out to God for guidance in a certain situation, but if we stubbornly hold onto our own desired outcome, we hinder our prayer communication. True surrender means letting go of our own desires and being willing to move in the direction God leads, even if it's not what we initially wanted. Often, it is this inability to let go and yield to God's will that dries up our sense of connection with Him. We might feel that God is far away when, in reality, we have left Him standing behind a door we refuse to fully open.

Practical Steps to Pray with Humility and Surrender

1. **Acknowledge God's Sovereignty**: Begin your prayers by recognizing and affirming God's supreme authority and wisdom.
2. **Release Control**: Consciously release your grip on the outcomes you desire, and entrust the situation entirely to God.
3. **Pray for Alignment with God's Will**: Ask God to align your heart with His will, even if it means changing your plans.
4. **Practice Gratitude**: Thank God for His guidance and care, trusting that His plans are for your good.
5. **Reflect on Past Experiences**: Remember times when surrendering to God's will led to positive outcomes, reinforcing your trust in Him.

Example Prayer of Humility and Surrender

> Heavenly Father, I come before You, acknowledging Your supreme authority and wisdom. I lay my worries and fears at Your feet, trusting that You are able and willing to take care of everything. Help me to release control and fully surrender

to Your will, even if it means changing my plans. Align my heart with Your desires and guide me in Your paths. Thank You for Your unwavering guidance and care. In Jesus' name, I pray. Amen.

By praying with humility and surrender, we open ourselves to God's guidance and experience a deeper connection with Him.

CHAPTER 25

The Importance of Silence and Listening in Prayer

The Nature of Prayer Dialogue

Prayer is often not a straightforward dialogue because our thoughts are not God's thoughts. It can sometimes feel like an argument, where our concerns are presented to God in a confused manner. At times, simply placing these concerns in God's presence without knowing how to express them is enough. Other times, we may encounter burdens that we later recognize as tasks entrusted to us by God. Ultimately, it is always God who initiates the dialogue through His Son, Jesus Christ, who is the very essence of our prayer dialogue. This underscores the power of prayer, leading us from darkness to light as we believe and hold onto Jesus, who is always by our side.

Finding God in Silence

When alone, we are always with ourselves, reminding us to turn within to find God present there. By being with God in the silence of prayer and remaining within Him at other times, we can experience the profound truth that God is nearer to us than we are to ourselves. In prayer, it is not just us praying but Christ within us. By faithfully remaining in this presence, we learn to experience Christ praying to the Father. Thus, prayer becomes a dialogue between God and man.

The Mystery of Silence

Silence in prayer is a profound mystery. It seems contradictory, yet those who have been in God's presence understand its significance. Concepts cannot fully capture the meaning of silence, as its true nature lies in profound openness to God. When the entire Church prays and worships, it should draw upon and live this silence to truly be in contact with God.

Practical Steps to Embrace Silence and Listening in Prayer

1. **Set Aside Quiet Time**: Dedicate specific times for silent prayer each day. This helps create a habit of quiet contemplation and listening.
2. **Focus on God's Presence**: In your silent moments, focus on the presence of God within you. Visualize being in His presence and open your heart to His guidance.
3. **Embrace Stillness**: Let go of distractions and allow yourself to be still. Silence your mind and soul to better hear God's voice.
4. **Reflect on Scripture**: Use passages from the Bible to meditate upon in silence. Let the words guide you into a deeper connection with God.
5. **Be Patient**: Listening in prayer requires patience. Give yourself the time and space to fully engage in silent communion with God.

Example Prayer for Embracing Silence

> **Heavenly Father, I come before You seeking to embrace the silence and to listen for Your voice. Help me to set aside**

time each day to be still in Your presence. Open my heart and mind to hear Your guidance and to experience Your nearness. Teach me to appreciate the mystery of silence and to find peace in Your presence. Thank You for always being near to me. In Jesus' name, I pray. Amen.

By incorporating silence and listening into your prayer life, you can deepen your spiritual connection and experience a more profound communion with God.

CHAPTER 26

Praying for God's Will to be Done

When Jesus taught His disciples how to pray, He emphasized the importance of praying for God's will to be done on earth as it is in heaven. This inclusion in the Lord's Prayer indicates that God's will being done is not automatic—it needs to be prayed for. Here are several reasons why praying for God's will to be done is crucial:

Understanding God's Will

1. **Uncertainty in Decisions**: We don't always know God's will in specific situations. Sometimes, two choices may seem right, but only one aligns perfectly with God's plan. Praying for His will helps us discern the correct path and prevents us from making rash decisions that could lead to sin.

2. **Alignment with Heaven**: God's will is always done in heaven. Our prayers should seek to align our lives with His perfect will on earth. This involves a continuous heart check, ensuring that our desires and actions are in line with God's purposes.

The Role of the Holy Spirit

The Holy Spirit plays a significant role in helping us understand and pray for God's will. The Spirit brings conviction about specific areas in our lives that need change and guides us to pray more fervently about those aspects. This divine guidance ensures that our prayers are not just personal desires but align with God's greater plan.

Practical Steps to Pray for God's Will

1. **Daily Surrender**: Begin each day by surrendering your plans and desires to God. Ask for His guidance and wisdom to align your actions with His will.

2. **Seek Biblical Guidance**: Regularly read and meditate on Scripture. The Bible provides insights into God's character and His will, helping you to pray in accordance with His word.

3. **Listen to the Holy Spirit**: Be attentive to the Holy Spirit's promptings. The Spirit often brings specific areas to mind that require prayer and adjustment.

4. **Pray for Discernment**: Continuously pray for the ability to discern God's will in various situations. Ask for clarity and wisdom to make decisions that honor Him.

5. **Be Open to God's Direction**: Approach prayer with an open heart, willing to accept and follow God's direction, even if it means changing your plans.

Example Prayer for God's Will

> Heavenly Father, I come before You, seeking to align my life with Your perfect will. Help me to understand and discern Your will in every situation. I surrender my plans and desires to You, asking for Your guidance and wisdom. Holy Spirit,

convict me of areas that need change and guide my prayers to align with God's purposes. Let Your will be done in my life as it is in heaven. In Jesus' name, I pray. Amen.

By consistently praying for God's will to be done and seeking alignment with His purposes, we can live lives that honor Him and fulfill His divine plan.

CHAPTER 27

Nurturing a Heart of Compassion through Prayer

Living at Peace with All

The directive to live at peace with everyone and to not repay evil with evil but with blessing is central to developing a heart of compassion (Romans 12:18, 1 Peter 3:9). This approach keeps even the most challenging individuals from taking residence in your heart. Practice this with patience and love, whether dealing with a difficult friend, an irritating relative, or even someone you hear about in the news.

Christ's Example

Reflect on Christ's conduct and be compelled by His immense love (1 John 4:7-12, 20-21). Jesus is the ultimate example of compassion, showing us how to love and serve others selflessly.

Love in Action

Compassion becomes tangible when we see it as a verb. The goal of the Christian life is to become more Christlike, and this is demonstrated through love in action. Peter reiterates this in 1 Peter 3:8-9, echoing Jesus' teachings from the Sermon on the Mount.

Praying for Compassion

Begin by acknowledging God's great mercy and love for you. Jonathan Edwards beautifully captured this sentiment: "When the heart is once prepared to see how great, how good, how sweet, how excellent Christ is, it cannot but melt with love to Him." Compassion is essentially love in action, and it is inspired by contemplating Jesus' love. Paul understood this well: "For Christ's love compels us" (2 Corinthians 5:14). The cross is the ultimate display of this love.

Practical Steps to Foster Compassion

1. **Daily Reflection**: Set a specific time each day to reflect on Christ's sacrifice, perhaps just before reading God's Word.
2. **Meditate on Scripture**: Begin with passages like John 20:2 or other gospel narratives. Let these scriptures move your heart and deepen your appreciation for Jesus' love.
3. **Practice Active Love**: Extend love through actions, especially towards those who may be difficult to love. This might involve acts of kindness, forgiveness, and understanding.
4. **Pray for Guidance**: Regularly ask God to fill your heart with compassion and to guide you in expressing His love to others.
5. **Serve Others**: Engage in acts of service, as serving others helps us emulate the compassion of our Father in Heaven.

Example Prayer for Compassion
> Heavenly Father, I come before You, acknowledging Your immense mercy and love. Help me to see how great and excellent Christ is, and let my heart be moved with love for Him. Fill me with Your compassion, and guide me to extend this love to others, even those who are difficult to love. As I reflect on Jesus' sacrifice, may I be compelled by His love to act with kindness, patience, and understanding. In Jesus' name, I pray. Amen.

By nurturing a heart of compassion through these practices, you can grow in Christlikeness and spread His love to those around you.

CHAPTER 28

Praying for the World and Global Issues

Focusing on God

Prayer for the world is centered on God, as it is from Him that we gain the strength to love, acknowledge pain, and find inspiration to act in harmony with Christ. This type of prayer engages all aspects of our being—body, soul, and spirit. The complexities and magnitude of global issues are beyond human capacity to resolve alone, and only by bringing these concerns to God in prayer can we release His power to address them.

The Importance of Global Prayer

Praying for the world is especially crucial in today's context. It starts with a conscious decision to recognize the sufferings of the world and our role in them. We must open our hearts, minds, and bodies to the distress of others, regardless of the personal cost. This commitment to sharing in the world's pain is a profound act of love, requiring us to continually turn to God and acknowledge the ongoing pain and suffering.

Practical Steps to Pray for Global Issues

1. **Acknowledge the Pain**: Begin by recognizing the immense suffering and challenges faced by people around the world. Allow yourself to feel compassion and empathy for those affected.

2. **Commit to Prayer**: Make a dedicated commitment to pray for global issues regularly. Set aside specific times to focus on these prayers.

3. **Educate Yourself**: Stay informed about global issues and understand the complexities involved. This knowledge will help you pray more specifically and effectively.

4. **Join Others in Prayer**: Participate in group prayers or join global prayer movements. Praying with others can amplify your efforts and bring a sense of community.

5. **Take Action**: Let your prayers inspire you to take action, whether through volunteering, supporting charities, or advocating for change.

Example Prayer for Global Issues

> **Heavenly Father, we come before You, acknowledging the immense suffering and pain faced by people around the world. We ask for Your strength and compassion to open our hearts to their distress. Help us to recognize our part in these issues and to seek Your guidance in addressing them. May Your power be released to bring healing, justice, and peace to those in need. Give us the wisdom and courage to act in harmony with Christ and to make a positive impact in the world. In Jesus' name, we pray. Amen.**

By committing to praying for global issues and allowing God to guide and inspire us, we can contribute to meaningful change and embody His love in a world in need.

Praying in Community and Fellowship

Challenges of Communal Prayer

Participating in communal prayer can sometimes be challenging. Some reasons might include:

- **Personal Discomfort**: Praying aloud in front of others can be intimidating.
- **Divergent Prayer Styles**: Differences in how people pray can lead to discomfort.
- **Time Constraints**: Finding a common time to gather and pray can be difficult.
- **Distractions**: External distractions or internal worries can disrupt communal prayer.

Making Communal Prayer a Regular Practice

To overcome these challenges and make communal prayer a regular part of spiritual life, consider these approaches:

- **Commit to Regular Times**: Establish fixed times during the day for communal prayer.

- **Create a Safe Space**: Ensure that the environment is welcoming and non-judgmental.
- **Utilize Common Prayers**: Use well-known prayers like the Lord's Prayer and the Collect to create a shared foundation.
- **Embrace Silence**: Integrate periods of silence to allow for personal reflection and listening to God's voice.
- **Discernment**: Practice discernment to navigate and address any difficulties that arise during communal prayer.

The Role of Silence

Silence plays a crucial role in communal prayer. It allows for:

- **Reflection**: Individuals can reflect on their thoughts and prayers.
- **Listening**: Silence provides an opportunity to listen for God's guidance.
- **Unity**: Shared silence can create a sense of unity and collective focus.

Common Forms of Prayer

Using common forms of prayer, such as the Lord's Prayer and the Collect, helps unify the group and provides structure. These prayers are familiar and can be a comforting foundation for communal prayer sessions.

Practical Guidance for Communal Prayer

1. **Establish Clear Intentions**: Set clear intentions for the prayer session, whether it's seeking guidance, offering praise, or interceding for others.

2. **Prepare the Space**: Ensure the prayer environment is conducive to focus and reflection. This might include dim lighting, comfortable seating, and minimal distractions.
3. **Encourage Participation**: Invite everyone to participate in their own way, whether through spoken prayer, silent reflection, or shared readings.
4. **Address Difficulties**: Be open to discussing any challenges that arise and find ways to address them constructively.
5. **Foster Inclusivity**: Make sure the prayer session is inclusive and respectful of different prayer styles and traditions.

Example Prayer for Communal Fellowship

> **Heavenly Father, we come together as a community to seek Your presence and guidance. Help us to overcome any challenges we face in communal prayer and to create a space that is welcoming and inclusive. Let our prayers be a true expression of our fellowship in the Body of Christ. May Your Spirit guide us, and may we find strength and unity in our shared time with You. In Jesus' name, we pray. Amen.**

By making communal prayer a regular part of spiritual life and addressing any challenges with practical solutions, we can deepen our fellowship and grow closer to God together.

CHAPTER 30

The Transformative Power of Prayer

Asking for the Right Thing
Understanding what to ask for in prayer involves discerning between what is truly good and what merely appears to be good. The state of our soul—whether it is oriented towards God or away from Him—determines whether something is beneficial or harmful for us. Our desires typically fall into three categories: riches, fame, or the kingdom of heaven. Given this, our prayers should focus on what draws us closer to God or prevents us from straying from Him, and only to the extent that they achieve this purpose.

The Purpose of Prayer

Often, prayer is seen as a way to petition God to act in specific ways or to alter the natural course of events for our benefit. However, the deeper purpose of prayer is to transform the character and outlook of the person praying. If this transformation is to be positive, the individual must always seek to pray for what aligns with God's will and enhances their spiritual growth, avoiding what St. Augustine refers to as 'idleness of spirit.'

Practical Steps for Transformative Prayer

1. **Discern True Good**: Reflect on whether your prayers align with seeking God's kingdom rather than personal gain. Aim to understand what is genuinely good for your soul.
2. **Align Desires with God's Will**: Ensure that your prayers reflect a desire to grow closer to God and to do His will.
3. **Continuous Self-Examination**: Regularly examine the state of your soul to understand what you need to pray for.
4. **Seek Spiritual Growth**: Focus on prayers that foster spiritual growth and development rather than temporal benefits.
5. **Avoid Idleness of Spirit**: Pray with intention and purpose, seeking to transform your character and outlook in alignment with God's will.

Example Prayer for Transformation
> **Heavenly Father, guide my heart and mind to seek only what aligns with Your will. Help me to discern what is truly good and to pray for things that draw me closer to You. Transform my character and outlook through prayer, and let my desires be centered on Your kingdom. Protect me from idleness of spirit and help me to pray with intention and purpose. In Jesus' name, I pray. Amen.**

By focusing our prayers on what aligns with God's will and promotes spiritual growth, we can experience the transformative power of prayer in our lives.

CHAPTER 31

Maintaining a Journal of Prayer

Steps to Start and Maintain a Prayer Journal

Keeping a prayer journal can significantly enrich your spiritual journey. Here's how you can start and maintain one:

1. **Date Each Entry**: Begin each entry with the date. This helps track your prayers over time and see how they evolve.
2. **Give Yourself a Title**: Create a title for each entry to focus your thoughts and attention. This could be a theme or the main point of your prayer.
3. **Include Scripture**: Write down a verse or two of Scripture. These can guide your prayers and provide a foundation for your communication with God.
4. **Ask for Guidance**: Begin your journaling session by asking the Lord to reveal what He wants to impress on your heart. This opens you up to God's guidance and insights.
5. **Write Out Prayers**: Conclude your entry by writing out your prayer. This serves as a reminder of what you have taken to God in prayer and allows you to reflect on it later.

6. **Track Ongoing Prayers**: Keep a record of ongoing prayers or matters as they develop. This can be a faith-building exercise as you see how God responds over time.

Throughout the Day

- **Jot Down Thoughts**: During the day, briefly note down thoughts, Scriptures, or petitions that come to mind. These can be quick reminders that you can revisit during your dedicated prayer time.
- **Raise to the Lord**: During your devotional time, bring these written notes to God in prayer. This helps ensure that nothing important slips through the cracks.

Tools for Your Prayer Journal

- **Notebook or Loose-Leaf Binder**: A physical journal can be a tactile way to record your prayers.
- **Computer or Digital Tools**: If you prefer digital, use a document or a note-taking app to keep track of your entries. Digital journals can be easily edited, searched, and organized.

Reviewing and Reflecting

Periodically review your prayer journal. Look back at how you prayed, what you prayed for, and how God answered. This can be incredibly encouraging and affirming, showing you the journey of your faith and God's faithfulness.

Example Entry Structure

Here's an example of how you might structure an entry:

Date: November 11, 2024 **Title**: Trusting in God's Plan **Scripture**: Jeremiah 29:11 - "For I know the plans I have for you," declares the Lord, "plans to prosper you and not to harm you, plans to give you hope and a future." **Prayer**: Heavenly Father, I come before You today trusting in Your perfect plan for my life. Help me to surrender my worries and fears to You, knowing that You have good plans for me. Guide me in my decisions and give me the strength to follow Your will. Thank You for Your constant love and faithfulness. In Jesus' name, I pray. Amen.

By maintaining a prayer journal, you can keep your prayer life fresh and stimulating, and see how God is working in your life.

CHAPTER 32

Conclusion: The Transformative Power of Prayer

In reflecting on the entirety of this book, the practice of a prayer retreat as suggested by Dr. Chalmers stands out as a significant approach to deepening one's spiritual life. Setting an appointment with God for an extended time of prayer and committing to it until you have truly prayed is a powerful practice. Although this might not be widely popular, it is worth considering. Would God not respond to a sincere seeker by granting deeper access to Himself?

Key Insights on Powerful Prayer

The author grapples with questions about what makes for a powerful practice of prayer and how to enhance the efficacy of our prayers. Reflecting on personal experiences and the teachings from this book, here are some key takeaways:

1. **Consistency and Commitment**: Committing to regular, extended times of prayer can deepen our spiritual connection and understanding.

2. **Sincerity and Seeking**: Sincere seeking and earnest prayer open doors to experiencing God's presence and guidance more profoundly.
3. **Reflective Practice**: Regularly considering our own practice of prayer and making necessary adjustments can lead to more powerful and meaningful prayers.

The Nature of Prayer

It's essential to correct the misconception that God only begins to act after we pray. In reality, God is always at work, preparing to respond to our prayers even before we utter them. The Bible, rich in teachings about prayer, does not prescribe one "right" way to pray. It provides various examples and instructions, leaving room for personal expression and preference.

- **Long or Short Prayers**: Both have their place, depending on the situation and intent.
- **Private or Public Prayers**: Each context serves a purpose in fostering a personal relationship with God and a communal spirit.
- **Structured or Free-Form Prayers**: Both can be meaningful; the key is to pray from the heart.

Essence of Prayer

The essence of prayer lies in receiving God's goodness and effectively accessing His presence through conversation. Prayer transforms us, aligning our hearts with God's will and drawing us closer to Him.

Final Thoughts

As you embark on your prayer journey, consider experimenting with different forms and practices of prayer. Reflect on your experiences and remain open to God's guidance. With increased faith and a willingness to seek God earnestly, you will find your prayer life becoming more powerful and transformative.